AF280903

A Little Book of Advent

Sarah Curtius

Bibliografische Information der Deutschen
Nationalbibliothek:
Die Deutsche Nationalbibliothek verzeichnet diese Publikation in der Deutschen Nationalbibliografie;
detaillierte bibliografische Daten sind im Internet über http://dnb.dnb.de abrufbar.

Herstellung und Verlag: BoD – Books on Demand,
Norderstedt

ISBN: 978-3-756-863-174

CONTENTS

Welcome to this little book about Advent!

In this book, we are going to look at all sorts of things to do with the Advent and Christmas period:

- the history of Christmas,

- a few Christmas songs,

- some British Christmas traditions

- some Christmas fairy tales,

- and a few Christmas puzzles.

I am British and the book looks mainly at British Christmas traditions. A traditional British Christmas is quite different to Christmas in Germany where I have lived for nearly 30 years. I hope you enjoy discovering things which are similar to your traditions, as well as those which are very different.

Some of the pages have QR codes and links which will take you to some extra content online.

Thank you for buying this book. I wish you happy reading and a lovely Advent!

Sarah Curtius

What is Advent?

1st December

It's the first day of December! Have you opened the first door on your Advent calendar and enjoyed a piece of chocolate? Maybe someone has made you a calendar with small gifts for every day. Or maybe you made one for someone else. Let's start our book by looking at some Advent traditions.

The word "Advent" comes from the Latin word *adventus* which means 'coming'. In the Christian tradition, it is a time to think about Jesus' birth but also his second coming in the future.

In the 6th century, fasting began after St Martin's Day on 11th November. St Martin's Day was celebrated by eating goose and other fatty foods. After that, monks fasted on weekdays until 6th January. This was sometimes called St Martin's Lent because, like Lent, the period of fasting before Easter, people fasted for 40 days. Later, the Advent period was reduced to about four weeks, starting on the Sunday between 27th November and 3rd December.

In the Middle Ages, in the north of England, poor women travelled around the villages with a small box during Advent. If people paid half a penny, they could look inside the box to see two figures – Mary and Jesus. It was bad luck not to see inside one of these boxes before Christmas Eve.

The idea that Advent was a time of fasting continued. Bakers in Germany developed a recipe for this time of year. It was a dry bread called 'stollen', made of flour, yeast, oil and water. The bread was dry and tasteless. In the

15th century, the Prince Elector Ernst of Saxony, wrote to the Pope to ask for special permission to use butter in the stollen. Five popes refused before Pope Innocent VIII sent the famous "Butter Letter" to the prince! Finally, the Saxonian bakers could use butter in the recipe … but only for the Prince Elector's stollen! Everyone else had to pay a fine for eating butter during the time of fasting.

They have always loved their stollen in Saxony. In 1730, August II the Strong had a giant stollen baked. It weighed 1.7 tonnes and they had to build a special oven to bake it and a special knife to cut it. A copy of this knife, which is 1.6 metres long, is used to cut the stollen in the festival which still takes place at the Christmas Fair in Dresden. The biggest stollen ever made was not baked in Dresden, though. The over 72-metre-long cake was baked by Lidl in the Netherlands in 2010.

Like stollen, many of the Advent traditions we celebrate today come from Germany. The first Advent wreath was created for children at a mission school in north Germany in the 19th century. The children kept asking how long it was until Christmas so Pastor Johann Hinrich Wichern stuck 20 small candles and four big ones to a wooden wheel. The small candles were for the days and the big ones for the four Advent Sundays.

The first advent calendars were made in Germany at the beginning of the 20th century. They had doors to open to show a small picture. The first chocolate calendars were made in the late 1950s. Now you can get Advent calendars with all sorts of things hiding behind the doors – gin, beer, perfume, Lego or other toys or even treats for your pet.

Christmas Vocabulary

2nd December

We are going to look at some of the vocabulary you need to talk about Christmas in English. The day that Christmas is celebrated in English-speaking countries is **Christmas Day**, 25th December. The day before is called **Christmas Eve** and the day afterwards is **Boxing Day**.

A week after Christmas, we celebrate the new year. People have parties on **New Year's Eve** and wake up with a hangover on **New Year's Day**! In Scotland, they call this holiday **Hogmanay** and both 1st and 2nd January are **bank holidays**.

In Advent, we hang up **decorations** or decorate the Christmas tree. On the tree, people hang **baubles** which are balls made of very thin glass. In the UK, you will often find people use **tinsel** for decoration. Tinsel is shiny strips all tied together to make a long rope. Another word we use at Christmas is **trimmings**. We **trim the tree** which means to decorate it but we also use the word trimmings for Christmas lunch. **Turkey with all the trimmings** means a dinner with turkey and all the other things, like vegetables, especially **Brussels sprouts**[1] and sauces (more about food on December 15th).

In English-speaking countries, **Father Christmas** comes in the night of the 24th December. Some people call him **Santa Claus**. They may hang some

---

1. Brussels sprouts = Rosenkohl

stockings[2] or socks at the end of their bed or on the **chimney**. Children are told that Father Christmas comes into the houses through the chimney. It's amazing he does not make more of a mess in the house!

Father Christmas travels on a **sleigh** or **sledge** which is pulled by **reindeer**. Before Christmas, he is helped by **elves**. An **elf** is a small person with magical powers. In pictures they often have pointy ears.

Some families have a **nativity scene**[3] which usually has Mary and Joseph and the baby Jesus who lies in a **manger**[4] . The manger is the container which the animals eat from. The figures stand in a **stable**[5] , the building where animals are kept. The nativity scene may also include some shepherds and sheep and the **Magi**, sometimes called **The Three Wise Men** or **The Three Kings**.

In the UK, **nativity plays** are a very important tradition and you can often see them at schools and churches. The children play the roles of Mary and Joseph, the shepherds, the angels and the Wise Men, and sometimes also some sheep, cows and donkeys!

At Christmas, people wish each other a **Merry Christmas** or **Happy Christmas**. You may also see other greetings, especially in Christmas cards. Because not everyone celebrates Christmas as a Christian holiday, some people write **Happy Holidays** or **Season's Greetings**.

It is also common to see Christmas written as **Xmas**. Some people do not like this because they say "it takes Christ out of Christmas". However, the Greek letter "X" was often used to mean Christ as it is the first letter of the name Christ.

---

2. stocking = Strumpf

3. nativity scene = Weihnachstkrippe

4. manger = Futterkrippe

5. stable = Stall

Evergreen

3rd December

Freshly cut evergreens is one of the most wonderful smells of Advent. While many trees lose their leaves in the winter, evergreens stay green. They have always been seen as a sign that spring will return after the dark months of winter.

Church records from the Middle Ages show that churches bought holly and ivy to decorate the churches at Christmas time. The famous carol "The holly and the ivy" explains the religious symbolism of the holly. The white flowers are for the purity of Mary, the red berries are for Jesus' blood and the prickly

holly - Ilex, Stechpalme

leaves remind us of the crown of thorns that soldiers put on Jesus' head before the crucifixion.

ivy - Efeu

In homes in the Middle Ages, spinning wheels were decorated with holly, ivy, laurel and yew branches to stop them being used during the Christmas period.

"Kissing boughs" were popular decoration in the Tudor period. These were two circles of greenery (holly, laurel, ivy and so on) placed inside one another to form a sphere. By the Georgian period, these spheres were decorated with apples, ribbons or paper flowers.

The tradition of decorating a tree at Christmas comes from Germany. It may have started with so-called "Paradise Plays" which were performed on the feast of Adam and Eve which was on 24th December. In the Bible story, Eve takes fruit from the Tree of Knowledge in the Garden of Eden. For the play, apples were hung in a fir tree. In 1419, a guild in Freiburg set up a fir tree and decorated it with apples, wafers, gingerbread and tinsel.

In the 17th century, the first Christmas tree market sold Christmas trees in Strasburg. German immigrants took the custom to America but it was pictures of the royal family with Queen Victoria, Prince Albert and their children decorating a Christmas tree which made Christmas trees popular throughout the world.

laurel - Lorbeer

In 1923, the first National Christmas Tree was put up outside the White House in Washington D.C. The tree was covered with 2,500 electric bulbs. The electricity companies hoped that this would encourage more people to buy more electric lights to use at home and so use more electricity.

In the 1960s, people in the UK and the USA started buying plastic Christmas trees which they could use year after year. Nowadays, in the UK, two out of three trees are artificial.

Every year since 1947, the people of Norway have given a 20-metre-tall tree to the UK to say thank you for their help in the Second World War. The tree is transported by ship and then lorry and is put up in Trafalgar Square in London at the beginning of December every year.

Midwinter Feasts

4th December

People in the northern hemisphere have always celebrated a feast in the middle of winter to remember that light and summer will return. Indeed, many Christmas traditions have their roots in ancient celebrations at this time of year.

We know that the **winter solstice**[1] was important for the Bronze Age people of Britain because of the stone circle at Stonehenge, where the sun rises over the tallest stone on this day.

In Rome, they celebrated the god Saturn with days of drinking and feasting, called the "Saturnalia". People gave each other gifts which is something we still do at Christmas. Roles were reversed and slaves ate and dressed as their masters usually did. There was also a tradition of "cross-dressing" where men dressed as women and women dressed as men. These traditions continued into the Middle Ages. On January 6th, people celebrated the last day of Christmas ("Twelfth Night") with women dressing as men and men as women, and servants acting like their masters.

When Roman Emperor Constantine became a Christian in the 4th century, he decided the birth of Jesus should be celebrated around this time. In 414 AD, the day was officially fixed as 25th December. Despite now being an official

---

1. winter solstice = Wintersonnenwende

church feast day, the celebrations did not change much. Even into the Middle Ages, Christmas was still a good excuse for a wild party.

In Norway, where the winters are especially dark, the Vikings celebrated the festival "Jul" (Yule). In England in the Middle Ages, people with big houses carried on the tradition of the Yule log. A big **log**[2] was brought into the home and set on fire. It burned for twelve days as they celebrated and, in some cases, the burned remains were kept to help light the Yule log in the following year. The Viking pagan traditions mixed with the new Christian religion and we got the twelve days of Christmas. Nowadays, we still have a Yule log but it is a cake in the shape of a log and covered in chocolate. Delicious!

Decorating the house with mistletoe is another Christmas tradition with ancient roots. The Romans saw it as a symbol of peace and love. Viking warriors from different tribes met under mistletoe and laid down their weapons. In many cultures, mistletoe was seen as a symbol of **fertility**[3]. In Victorian times, it was tradition for a man to kiss a woman under mistletoe. If she agreed, one of the berries was picked off. When the berries were all gone, there was no more kissing! It was said, the woman would have bad luck, if she said no.

As we look at different Christmas customs, we will see some turning up again and again. The period at the darkest time of the year is a time when people always enjoyed parties and drinking. Cross-dressing is also something which we will see again and again. Throughout the ages, the Church usually found the celebrating too colourful and, as we will see, at one point they even banned Christmas!

Compared to Christmas celebrations in other countries in Europe which are often more serious, a British Christmas still involves parties and fun.

---

2. log = Holzstamm

3. fertility = Fruchtbarkeit

Elves and the Shoemaker by The Brothers Grimm

5th December

"T he Elves and the Shoemaker" is a fairy story written by Jacob and William Grimm and published in 1876 in a collection of stories called "Grimm's Goblins".

Once upon a time there was a shoemaker who worked very hard but was still very poor. He was so poor that he could only buy one last piece of leather to make a pair of shoes. He cut the shoes and laid them out, ready to sew them the next morning. Then the shoemaker went to bed.

In the morning, he came into his workshop to find that the shoes had already been made. He looked at them carefully and could see that they were very well sewn.

Later that day, a customer came into the shop and liked the shoes so much that he paid a higher price than normal for them. The shoemaker went out and bought the leather for two more pairs of shoes. He cut them out and left them ready to sew the next morning.

In the morning, he woke up to find that the same thing had happened again. There were two beautifully sewn shoes. Once again, he sold the shoes for a very good price and bought more leather for four more pairs of shoes. He laid them out and the next morning they had been sewn.

This went on for some time and slowly the shoemaker began to make enough money to support himself and his wife.

One evening near Christmas, he told his wife that he wanted to stay up and see who was sewing his shoes for him. That night, the shoemaker and his wife hid in the workshop and waited. At midnight, two naked little elves climbed up onto the table and started to sew the shoes which the shoemaker had left out. They worked so quickly and skilfully and by morning the shoes were finished and the elves left again.

When they were gone, the shoemaker's wife said how sorry she was to see these poor little creatures who had helped them so much. "They must be so cold in the winter," she said. "I'll make them each a shirt, a coat and a pair of trousers. You make them each a pair of shoes."

When the clothes were ready, the shoemaker and his wife laid them out on the table instead of the leather for the shoes. Then they hid to see what the elves would do. At midnight, the two little elves came into the workshop and climbed up on the table to start sewing. However, instead of the leather, they found the tiny clothes the shoemaker's wife had made for them. They were so happy. They put on the clothes and danced around the workshop. They put on the tiny shoes which the shoemaker had made and then they left the shoemaker's shop.

The shoemaker and his wife never saw the little elves again but their shop went from strength to strength and they lived happily ever after.

Saint Nicholas

6th December

Today is the saint's day of St Nicholas of Myra. Although the day is still celebrated in parts of Europe (mostly in the Netherlands, parts of Belgium, France, Germany and the Czech Republic), he is mostly forgotten in the English-speaking world, replaced by the figures of Father Christmas and Santa Claus.

Though there are many stories about St Nicholas and his generous and miraculous deeds, we do not know many details about his life. We know that he was born towards the end of the 3rd century (around 270), probably in a large town called Patara in **Asia Minor**[1] (modern-day Turkey). His parents were wealthy Greek Christians. His uncle was the bishop of Myra, another town in the same province of Asia Minor. After his uncle died, Nicholas became bishop of Myra.

Many of the stories about St Nicholas talk about his **generosity**[2] . After his parents died, he gave away all their money to the poor. One very famous story tells us of a man who had three daughters. He had once been rich but had

---

1. Asia Minor = Kleinasien

2. generosity = Großzügigkeit

lost all his money. He could now no longer afford the **dowries**[3] for his three daughters to be able to marry. St Nicholas heard about this and decided to help. He was too **humble**[4] to help them publicly, so he went to the house in the night and threw a purse filled with gold coins through the open window. As a result, the first daughter was able to marry. On the very night of her wedding, St Nicholas threw a second bag of gold through the window. After the second daughter was married, the father stayed awake to catch the secret helper. When St Nicholas came to deliver the third bag of gold, the father fell on his knees and thanked him. St Nicholas told him to keep the gifts a secret.

St Nicholas is also the patron saint of sailors. Some say that in the Middle Ages, all the sailors of the Low Countries (the Netherlands) would go to the harbour towns for a church celebration of their patron saint. At the time, almost all the men in the Low Countries were either active or retired sailors. On their way back home, they would stop at 'St Nicholas fairs' to buy small gifts for their families. Proper presents were given at Christmas but these little gifts 'from St Nicholas' were given straight away.

It is probably stories like these about secret gift giving as well as the stories about St Nicholas' kindness to children that led to St Nicholas being celebrated as a bringer of gifts, especially in the Netherlands. Dutch settlers brought their traditions of 'Sinterklaas' with them to America where they **merged**[5] with British colonialists' stories about Father Christmas to eventually give us 'Santa Claus'.

Text by Iona Curtius

---

3. dowry = Mitgift

4. humble = demütig

5. to merge - verschmelzen; in einander übergehen

Cancel Christmas!

7th December

In the Middle Ages, Christmas was a twelve-day-long party. The "Lord of Misrule" was the person in charge of these medieval parties. He organised games and these could be rough. One of the games was called "Hot Cockles". One person was **blindfolded**[1] and then had to guess who had slapped them. If they guessed correctly, the other person was blindfolded.

Everyone ate and drank special food at Christmas time. **Boar**[2] was very popular but if you were rich, you ate **pasties**[3] and sausages, too. This was followed by nuts and sweet things like tarts and custard. The people in the Middle Ages also liked their alcoholic drinks. While the poorer people drank spiced ale or cider, the rich drank wine. And they drank A LOT of wine. The records show that for one Christmas, Henry V ordered 60 tons of wine. That is more than 76,000 bottles!

There was an old tradition called **wassailing** where people went from house to house singing songs and sharing a bowl of warm spiced ale or wine. The word "wassail" comes from a Viking word which meant "to be in good

---

1. blindfolded = mit verbundenen Augen

2. boar = Wildschwein

3. pasties = Pasteten

health". The phrase was used as a toast when people enjoyed a drink together. The phrase is similar to toasts in other languages. **Santé** in French, **Salud** in Spanish and **Sláinte** in Irish all mean "health". In the Middle Ages, poor people went to the landowner's house at Christmas time and sang carols. The landowner then invited them in and gave them something to eat and drink. Christmas was a good time for working people. No-one could force a free man to work during the twelve days of Christmas in the Middle Ages.

In the 16th century, people still enjoyed Christmas parties and dressing up. At Henry VIII's court, the king and his men dressed up as Robin Hood or as Moors and the others pretended that they did not recognise them. On Twelfth Night (6th January), the people ate a special cake which had a bean baked into it. Whoever got the piece of cake with the bean was "King of the Bean". This meant that for the rest of the evening, everyone else had to copy whatever the "King" did. If the king ate, then they would eat and if the king drank, then they would drink.

The Tudors gave each other presents not at Christmas, but on New Year's Day. The most important feature of Christmas food in Tudor times was sugar. The Tudors loved their sugar. There were sugar models of castles and they even made drinking cups out of sugar. Elizabeth I loved sugar so much that it turned her teeth black.

With all this wild partying, it is not surprising that the Puritans wanted to put a stop to it. In Scotland, the Reformer John Knox had already banned all Church festivals. When Oliver Cromwell and the Puritans took over the Parliament in England, they made laws to completely ban celebrations of saints' days and Christmas. In 1647, the people protested against the law in London and other English towns and people even died in the riots in Ipswich. Despite the ban, people all over the country celebrated in secret. When the monarchy was restored in 1660, Christmas was also restored and people could celebrate it in England once again. In Scotland, however, Christmas Day did not become a public holiday until 1871.

Christmas Cards

8th December

Robins, nativity scenes, Santa Claus, candles and snow scenes – these are all things you might see on a Christmas card. Do you write Christmas cards?

In the UK, people used to write lots of Christmas cards. When I first moved to Germany, people could not believe how many Christmas cards we got every year. It was sometimes over 100!

The first Christmas card was designed by John Callcott Horsley for Sir Henry Cole in 1843. Three years earlier, Cole had introduced the Penny Post. Since post could now be transported with the railway, more post could be transported and it became possible for more people to use the postal service. When the price to send a letter sank to half a penny in 1870, writing cards became even more popular.

About 160 countries now **issue**[1] special Christmas stamps for you to stick on your Christmas post. The first stamp with a nativity scene was issued in 1943 in Hungary. By the 1960s, many other countries had started designing special Christmas themed stamps.

Sending Christmas cards has become more expensive with the price of postage rising in the past years. Two old friends in the UK decided to reduce

---

1. to issue = herausgeben

the cost by re-using the same card for more than 50 years! One of the men sent the card to his friend in 1969, asking him to send it back by 1st December 1970. The pair have been writing a new message and sending it back and forth ever since. There is not a lot of space left on the card now, but they plan to keep up with their tradition for as long as possible.[2]

Although, they do not write as many as before, Brits still send more Christmas cards than any other nation The average Brit sends 17 Christmas cards. The Royal Mail say that they deliver about 150 million Christmas cards every year. Writing Christmas cards is more personal than a quick email and making your own Christmas cards makes it even more special.

You can find some easy ideas for making Christmas cards on my blog:

https://sarahcurtiusbooks.wordpress.com/christmas-cards/

---

2. Watch an interview with the men here:
   https://www.bbc.com/news/av/uk-england-hereford-worcester-50898386

Bah Humbug! A Victorian Christmas

9th December

During the Georgian period, Christmas once again became a time for parties and family gatherings. In a number of her books, Jane Austen describes Christmas balls with dancing and good food.

After the Puritans had banned it during the Republic, Christmas pudding made a comeback in the 18th century. It is said that George I was served Christmas pudding for his Christmas lunch and loved it so much that it became the official pudding for Christmas. This story is probably not true but it is the reason that he is nicknamed "the Pudding King".

George III's wife, Queen Charlotte introduced the German tradition of the Christmas tree to the royal household, but it was not until the times of Queen Victoria that normal people started bringing them into their homes.

In 1848, a newspaper printed a picture of the Queen with her husband Prince Albert standing around a Christmas tree and it was during Victoria's reign that Christmas became the holiday we celebrate in the UK today. Christmas trees and decorations, Christmas cards and Christmas crackers all started in the 19th century.

The tree in the royal palace was decorated with brightly coloured sweets and decorations which reflected in the candlelight. The first advertisements for sparkly decorations appeared in 1853 and together with candles, they were very popular.

The railways made it possible for people to travel from towns and cities to visit family who still lived in the countryside. Technology and mass production made gifts like children's toys cheaper and so more people could afford them.

While poor people did not have to work at Christmas time in the Middle Ages, in the Industrial Era, conditions for the poor were bad and most people had to work on Christmas Day. In Victoria's reign, there was a growing middle class who had enough money to celebrate Christmas and wanted to copy the ideal of the family Christmas they saw Victoria and Albert enjoying.

One person who made sure that Christmas would continue to be celebrated was Charles Dickens. In 1843, Dickens published his book "A Christmas Carol". It is a story about a cruel man called Scrooge who does not want to give his employee a day off at Christmas and just says, "Bah Humbug!". Scrooge receives a visit from the ghost of his dead business partner who warns him that he must change. In the night he will have three more ghostly visitors. First comes the Ghost of Christmas Past. The Ghost takes Scrooge back to his childhood and youth and we begin to understand why Scrooge has become so mean and unhappy. Next, we meet the Ghost of Christmas Present who is a jolly person based on the Father Christmas figure of old English folklore. This ghost shows Scrooge the family of his employee Bob Cratchit and we see their son Tiny Tim who is very ill. Finally, Scrooge has a visit from the Ghost of Christmas Yet to Come. This ghost does not speak to Scrooge but shows him his death and the fact that no-one will cry for him when he is gone.

When Scrooge wakes up the next morning, he is a changed man. He hurries to Bob Cratchit's home and buys them Christmas dinner. He is kind and generous, gives money to a charity and becomes a father figure to Tiny Tim.

The book became Dickens' most popular story and has been adapted into plays and films. Dickens' book reflects the change in how people were beginning to celebrate Christmas in the 19th century. We see how important it was to spend time with family, to enjoy Christmas dinner with Christmas pudding and the importance of being generous and supporting charities which continues today.

Christmas Carols

10th December

C arol is another word which you only hear at Christmas. Singing Christmas carols is still a popular way to prepare for Christmas.

Originally, a "carol" was a joyful song which people danced to. The earliest collection of Christmas carols is from 1521. It was printed by a man called Wyncken de Worde. He came to England from Germany and took over the first printing business in England which had been started by William Caxton. In his lifetime, Wyncken printed over 800 editions of 400 different books. Caxton was supported by rich people and royalty but Wyncken made the business into a printing press for the people. He moved the business to Fleet Street which was to become the centre of printing and publishing in London. He was the first to use *italics* in his books and the first to print musical notes in a book. He was also the first person to set up a book stall at St Paul's Cathedral which became the centre for bookselling in London. Only one page of Wyncken's collection of Christmas carols has **survived**[1]. The carol is called "Boar's Head Carol" and describes a boar's head being carried into a Christmas feast.

Singing carols was very popular throughout the Middle Ages and into Tudor times. Martin Luther wrote a number of carols and the Lutheran Reformers

---

1. to survive = überleben

encouraged[2] carol singing. However, the Calvinist Reformers did not approve of Christmas celebrations, including singing carols. During the period of the Republic in England, it was forbidden to celebrate Christmas.

As we have already seen, the Victorians "re-discovered" Christmas and many of the carols sung in the UK today are from the late 19th century. Most Victorian carols are about the birth of Jesus but often the carols tell us more about the time they were written in than the Christmas story. For 200 years, from the middle of the 17th century, the earth experienced a "Mini Ice Age". The winters were very cold and there was plenty of snow. In London, the Thames often froze over.

Jesus was born in 1st century Palestine, and probably in the spring not the winter. So, Christina Rossetti's famous poem certainly describes life in London in the 19th century rather than the time of Jesus' birth in Bethlehem. However, it is a beautiful poem, set to music and still sung as a carol.

> In the bleak midwinter, frosty wind made moan,
> Earth stood hard as iron, water like a stone;
> Snow had fallen, snow on snow, snow on snow,
> In the bleak midwinter, long ago. [...]

> What can I give Him, poor as I am?
> If I were a shepherd, I would bring a lamb;
> If I were a Wise Man, I would do my part;
> Yet what I can I give Him: give my heart.

---

2. to encourage = ermutigen

THE TWELVE DAYS OF CHRISTMAS

11TH DECEMBER

This famous Christmas carol is fun to sing. It is a list of all the things that a man sends to his "true love".

The carol was first published in 1780 but it is believed to be much older. After Henry VIII took the English church out of the Church in Rome, Catholics in England were persecuted. Some people believe that the song was used by Catholics to teach their beliefs secretly and the gifts have special meanings. The partridge in the pear tree is Jesus, the three French hens are the Holy Trinity (God the Father, Son and Holy Spirit), the four calling birds are the four gospels, and so on.

If you like maths puzzles, perhaps you would like to work out how many gifts are included in the carol. It depends whether on the second day, he gives his love just two turtle doves or two turtle doves plus another partridge in a pear tree, and so on. It also depends on whether you count the partridge and the pear tree as one or two gifts.

Every year, the PNC Christmas Price Index[1] works out how much it would cost to give all these gifts. In 2021, it worked out that it would cost over US $41,000. This was nearly 6% more than the year before.

---

1. https://www.pncchristmaspriceindex.com/

Here is the text of the carol:

> On the first day of Christmas, my true
> love sent to me
> A partridge in a pear tree.
> On the second day of Christmas, my
> true love sent to me
> Two turtle doves and a partridge in a
> pear tree.

and so on until the last verse:

> On the twelfth day of Christmas, my
> true love sent to me
> Twelve drummers drumming,
> eleven pipers piping,
> ten lords a-leaping,
> nine ladies dancing,
> eight maids a-milking,
> seven swans a-swimming,
> six geese a-laying,
> five golden rings;
> four calling birds,
> three French hens,
> two turtle doves
> and a partridge in a pear tree.

POINSETTIA

12TH DECEMBER

A s well as evergreen wreaths and candles, the **poinsettia**[1] is a very popular plant used for decoration at Christmas time. The plant has green and red leaves with small yellow flowers.

Poinsettias come from Mexico where they can grow up to four metres high. The Aztecs used the red leaves to make a **dye**[2] for clothes. You may have noticed that, if you break off a leaf, the plant loses a milky **sap**[3]. This is **slightly poisonous**[4] and can cause problems if you get it in your eyes. The Aztecs used this sap for medicine to lower a fever.

There is an old Mexican legend about the plant. A poor Mexican girl called Pepita was going to the Christmas Eve service at church but she was sad because she did not have a present to bring for the baby Jesus. Her cousin Pedro tried to cheer her up and said, "It doesn't matter how big the gift is. If Jesus sees that you love him, it will make him happy."

---

1. poinsettia = Weihnachtsstern

2. dye = Farbstoff

3. sap = Pflanzensaft

4. slightly poisonous = geringfügig giftig

Pepita picked some **weeds**[5] on the way to church and tried to make them look pretty. When she got to church, she walked to the front of the church and put them down on front of the nativity scene. Suddenly big red flowers appeared among the weeds. The people in the church were amazed by the miracle and called it "The Flowers of the Holy Night".

European travellers discovered the plant in the early 19th century. It was the first U.S. **ambassador**[6] to Mexico who started sending poinsettia plants back to his home in California. His name was Joel Roberts Poinsett and he gave the poinsettia its name.

70 million poinsettias are sold every year in the U.S. alone. Half of all of the poinsettias sold worldwide are grown by the Paul Ecke Ranch which now grows them in Guatemala. Paul Ecke was a German immigrant who started growing plants in Los Angeles and selling them from street stalls. If poinsettias are left to grow on their own, they grow tall and thin, but Paul Ecke worked out how to grow them so that grew thicker and were more attractive. His grandson made poinsettias popular by giving them to American TV shows between Thanksgiving and Christmas. By 1986, the poinsettia was the best-selling potted plant in America.

December 12th is National Poinsettia Day. It is the day of ambassador Poinsett's death. The day was created by U.S. Congress in 2002 to **honour**[7] Paul Ecke Jr. who made the poinsettia so popular. There are now 100 different varieties of the plant and you can buy them with white, yellow, pink or patterned leaves.

---

5. weed(s) = Unkraut

6. ambassador = Botschafter

7. to honour = ehren

Christmas Statistics

13th December

T oday we are looking at some Christmas statistics. Match the numbers with the clues.

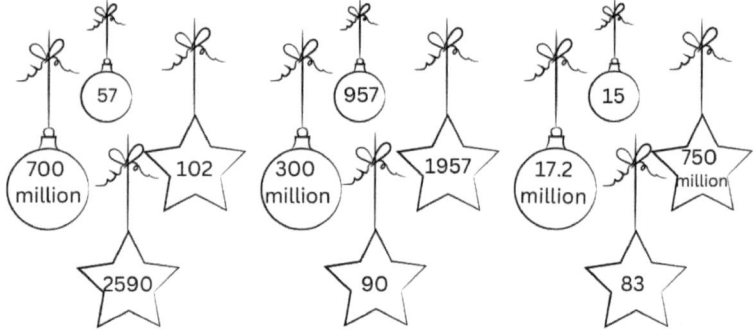

Preparing for Christmas

1. This is the percentage of people in the UK who put up a tree in their house at Christmas time.

2. If those people put up a real Christmas tree, the average age of that tree will be ….. years.

3. In square kilometres, how much wrapping paper is bought to wrap Christmas presents?

4. In British pounds, how much is spent on gifts that people do not actually want?

CHRISTMAS DAY

1. King George VI began the tradition of giving a speech on the radio on Christmas Day in 1932. In which year did Queen Elizabeth II make the first speech on the television?

2. Is Christmas Day a good day to get married? How many weddings took place in the UK between 1996 and 2015?

3. It seems that some people get bored on Christmas Day. How many people submitted their tax returns online on Christmas Day 2017?

EATING AND DRINKING

1. How many Brussels sprouts are sold around Christmas in the UK?

2. How many of the Brussels sprouts are thrown away?

3. How many **mince pies**[1] are eaten at Christmas in the UK?

4. How many calories are in a traditional British Christmas Dinner?

5. If you added up all the beer drunk at Christmas, how many Olympic-sized pools would it fill?

Find the answers here: https://sarahcurtiusbooks.wordpress.com/christmas-statistics/

---

1. mince pies = sweet pies filled with dried fruit

Pantomime – Christmas Entertainment

14th December

In every British town and city, you will find a theatre performing a Pantomime at Christmas time. Some are performed by amateur groups but in large towns and cities, there are big productions with famous actors playing the parts. Pantomimes are popular with young and old. They have songs and dancing, comedy and romance. The audience is encouraged to get involved, sing and shout. Let's take a look at another very British Christmas custom!

Pantomimes are usually versions of fairy tales. Popular pantomimes are Cinderella, Aladdin, Snow White and also English fairy tales like Dick Whittington and Jack and the Beanstalk.

Once again, this tradition involves cross-dressing with men dressed as women and women dressed as men. The pantomime also has elements of the commedia dell'arte, a type of improvised play from Italy. It had so-called "stock characters" who were either completely good or completely bad.

A modern pantomime has a "Pantomime Dame" which is a man dressed up as an older woman and a "Principal Boy", usually the main male character who is played by a young woman. There is an evil villain who is booed by the audience and a good character like a good fairy who the audience loves. When the villain appears, the audience shout and warn the good characters by shouting, "He's behind you!" There is always a lot of music, often with new words written for well-known tunes. Children love the jokes and the slapstick but there are usually some jokes especially for the adults, too.

One of the most popular pantomimes is the English fairy tale **Jack and the Beanstalk**. The story starts with Jack (often played by a girl) and his mother (the pantomime dame) who are very poor. They have a cow, a "pantomime cow", played by two actors in a costume, one as the head and front legs and one as the body and back legs. The cow is old and does not give them any milk so Jack takes the cow to market. No one wants to buy a cow which does not give any milk, so Jack sets off home again.

On the way, Jack meets a man who wants to buy the cow for five magic beans. Jack accepts the offer but when he gets home, his mother is very angry. She throws the beans into the garden for the birds.

The next morning, Jack wakes up to find a huge beanstalk has grown in the garden. He climbs the beanstalk far into the sky and at the top he finds a castle. He knocks the door and it is opened by a giant woman. Jack rushes inside.

Soon the woman's husband (the villain) comes home and says, "Fee-fi-fo-fum! I smell the blood of an Englishman!" The giant sits down and eats a meal and then he counts his money – 100 silver coins. While the giant is asleep, Jack takes the money and climbs back down the beanstalk.

He shares the money with the other poor people in his village and soon the money is all gone. Jack decides to go back up the beanstalk to the giant's castle and this time he finds that the giant has a magic hen which lays golden eggs. Jack steals the hen and climbs back down the beanstalk.

The people live from the money from the golden eggs for a long time but when it is stolen, Jack decides to go back to the castle one more time. This time, he finds a magic harp. As Jack tries to steal the harp, the harp speaks and warns the giant. The giant wakes and chases Jack down the beanstalk. At the bottom, Jack's mother is waiting with an axe. Jack cuts down the beanstalk and the giant falls to his death.

At the end of the story, the magic hen has been found and even the cow has come home again!

CHRISTMAS FOOD

15TH DECEMBER

In the UK, the traditional meal for Christmas Day is **turkey** with all the trimmings. Turkeys come from America and were introduced to Britain around 1523. King Henry VIII was one of the first to eat it and soon it became popular throughout the country. A Royal Tudor Christmas lunch included turkey, stuffed with a goose, stuffed with a chicken, stuffed with a partridge, stuffed with a pigeon, in a pastry case!

Most turkeys are still bred in Norfolk in the east of England. In the 19th century, before the railways, it was difficult to get them to London for Christmas. The turkeys had to walk 100 miles and the farmers made little leather boots to protect their feet. Geese, on the other hand, did not like wearing the boots so the farmers dipped their feet in soft tar before they set off on their long hike.

"All the trimmings" means, among other things, stuffing, gravy, cranberry sauce, pigs in blankets (sausages wrapped in bacon), roast potatoes and vegetables, especially parsnips, carrots and Brussels sprouts.

After the main meal, we eat **Christmas pudding**. This started off as a kind of thick vegetable soup called pottage with some added dried fruit, spices and wine and it was eaten at the beginning of the meal. It was sometimes called "figgy pudding". In the Christmas carol "We wish you a merry Christmas", for example, in one of the verses the people sing, "So, bring us some figgy pudding!".

By the end of the 17th century, the figgy pudding or plum pudding had become more solid and was sliced and eaten together with roasted meat. In the 19th century, the pudding became the traditional dessert after Christmas dinner.

The Victorians established the tradition of "Stir Up Sunday". On the fifth Sunday before Christmas, the family made their Christmas pudding. Every family member stirred the mixture from east to west to remember the journey of the Wise Men. A coin or other small objects were baked in the pudding and either brought good or bad luck to the person who found them on Christmas Day.

Modern Christmas pudding contains raisins and spices and is steamed, rather than baked in the oven. Before it is served, you pour brandy over it and set it alight! It is eaten with custard or a sweet sauce called **brandy butter**.

My favourite food for the Christmas period is **mince pies**. In the Middle Ages, they included dried fruit, spices, suet (beef fat) and mutton. There were thirteen ingredients as a symbol for Jesus and his disciples. The pies were made in the shape of a baby's bed with a baby Jesus on top. This was the reason that the Puritans banned the pies.

Nowadays, mince pies no longer contain meat, although they sometimes still have suet in them, which is fat from beef. They are made with raisins, chopped apple and chopped citrus peel, nuts, spices (cinnamon, cloves and nutmeg) and often brandy or rum. They are served warm and sometimes with cream or brandy butter.

And what about traditional drinks at Christmas? **Mulled wine**, warm wine with spices like cinnamon, aniseed and cloves, is common. Another traditional drink is **eggnog**. This is made with eggs, milk, cream and rum or a whisky blend.

Christmas Day Events

16th December

There are many interesting events that took place on Christmas Day. Here are just two which happened in Westminster Abbey.

Coronation of William I

In 1066, William of Normandy **invaded**[1] England. He defeated the Saxon king Harald and became William I, William the Conqueror. On Christmas Day that year, he was crowned in Westminster Abbey. Christmas Day was a popular day for coronations in the Middle Ages. In 800, Charlemagne, the great Emperor of the Holy Roman Emperor was crowned by the Pope in Aachen.

The situation in London in 1066 was tense. The Anglo-Saxons did not trust their new Norman king. At the end of the service, there were cheers from inside the abbey. William's soldiers thought it was a riot and set the buildings around the abbey on fire. The people in the abbey panicked and William and the priests were left alone to finish the coronation.

The Stone of Destiny

For centuries, Scottish kings were crowned on a large stone called "The Stone of **Destiny**[2] ". The stone is a 152kg piece of sandstone. It was very

---

1. to invade = überfallen; in ein Land einmarschieren

2. destiny = Schicksal

important to the Scots and was stolen from Scone Abbey in 1296 by the Norman King Edward I who took it to London. Edward had the stone fitted into the coronation chair in Westminster Abbey. In the 14th century, one English King promised the King of Scotland that he would return the stone but it remained in London for another 600 years.

That is until Christmas Day in 1950. Four Scottish students broke into the Abbey in the night and took the stone from underneath the coronation chair. As they did so it broke into two pieces. They took both pieces to their cars outside the Abbey. They buried the big piece of the stone in Kent and went back to Scotland. When the police realised that the stone was missing, they closed the border between England and Scotland. It was the first time this had happened for 400 years.

Two weeks later the students returned and took the stone back to Scotland where they repaired it. On 11th April 1951, they put the stone on the High Altar in Arbroath Abbey and in February 1952, it was taken back to London.

All four of the students were interviewed by police and all but the organiser, Ian Hamilton, admitted to being involved. However, the police decided not to **prosecute**[3]. The idea of Scottish **devolution**[4] was not popular at the time but the theft of the stone made people think about it.

In 1996, 700 years after it was stolen by Edward I, the stone was given back to Scotland. It is now kept in Edinburgh Castle with the Scottish Crown Jewels.

In September 2022, it was announced that the stone would travel back to Westminster Abbey for the coronation of Charles III.

---

3. to prosecute = strafrechtlich verfolgen

4. devolution = Übertragung begrenzter parlamentarischer Gewalt und administrativer Unabhängigkeit

CHRISTMAS CRAFT: CHRISTINGLE

17TH DECEMBER

I t is just after four o'clock and the sun has set. Time to light a candle and sit down with a cup of tea and maybe a good book. Lighting a candle is one of the great joys of this time of year. For some, they are a symbol of God's light coming in the darkness. Others just enjoy the atmosphere of a flickering flame when it is cold and dark outside.

There is a special tradition which is often celebrated with a church service at Advent in the UK – a Christingle service.

It is believed that, like so many Christmas traditions, the Christingle tradition started in Germany. In an Advent service in 1747 in Marienborn, the Moravian minister Johannes de Watteville gave the children a candle with a piece of red ribbon wrapped around it. The candle symbolised the light of God and the red ribbon symbolised the blood of Jesus. At the end of the service, Watteville prayed that God would keep the light burning in the hearts of the children.

The tradition of giving children a candle and a red ribbon continued in the Moravian church and spread throughout the world.

In the 1960s, John Pensom thought he could use the idea of the Christingle to raise money for the charity he worked for. John worked for the Children's Society which is a charity in the UK which helps children who are poor or have got involved in crime. John decided to change the Christingle a little. He stuck the candle in an orange and used little sticks to fix sweets to the orange, too.

Other people did not like his idea and did not believe it would help raise money. However, it has become very popular. Every year, churches all over the United Kingdom hold Christingle services and millions of pounds have been raised to help children. In Northern Ireland especially, it has been a great chance to bring people together.

The modern Christingle still has a special meaning:

- the orange represents the world,

- the red ribbon is Jesus' blood,

- the sweets represent all of creation, and

- the candle is Jesus' light which came into the world at Christmas.

For more information on the Christingle campaign and how to make one, go to https://www.childrenssociety.org.uk/how-you-can-help/fundraise-and-events/christingle/what-is-christingle

CHRISTMAS CRACKERS

18TH DECEMBER

C hristmas crackers are a very British Christmas tradition. Before the meal on Christmas Day, the family pull at the brightly wrapped tubes which they find lying on their plates. When pulled, there is a bang and out fall three things: a paper crown, a piece of paper with a joke and a small gift. The paper crown must be worn by everyone for the Christmas lunch. Then people take it in turns to read their jokes. These usually involve a play on words which cause most of the family members to **groan**[1] rather than laugh. The gift is often something like a pair of **nail clippers**[2] , a pen or a **tape measure**[3] .

So, where did this strange tradition come from?

Like so many Christmas traditions, it started with the Victorians. A sweet maker called Tom Smith had the idea and sold the first crackers in the 1860s. On a trip to Paris, Smith had seen "bon-bons", small sweets wrapped in colourful paper. He tried selling them in England and added a riddle or a short motto, but they did not sell well.

---

1. to groan = stöhnen

2. nail clippers = Nagelknipser

3. tape measure = Maßband

Tom had the idea of adding a tiny firework which made a bang when you pulled the sweet paper apart and suddenly the crackers started to sell. After Tom's death, his three sons took over the business and they introduced the paper crown and the small gift.

They started making special crackers. They made crackers especially for Suffragettes and for War Heroes and for single people with fake wedding rings and false teeth!

Even though the jokes are terrible and the presents usually cheap and useless, Christmas crackers are an important part of a British Christmas lunch and I wouldn't miss them for the world!

Here are some of those terrible Christmas cracker jokes:

Why is Turkey popular at Christmas?
Because it's warmer there.

What did the Christmas bell say to the other Christmas bell?
Give me a ring sometime.

What is Tarzan's favourite Christmas song?
Jungle Bells

Why are Christmas trees so bad at sewing?
They keep dropping their needles.

What did the sea say to Santa?
Nothing! It just waved!

What do you call an elf wearing ear muffs?
Anything you like, they can't hear you!

1914 Christmas Truce

19th December

"**O**ver by Christmas!"

That is what people thought when the First World War started in 1914. By December 1914, the war was not over and life in the **trenches**[1] was hard. It was cold and wet and the soldiers could not spend Christmas with their families. The Pope had said there should be no fighting at Christmas but the generals ignored his wish. However, in some places fighting did stop for a few days.

The German soldiers had small Christmas trees in the trenches. On Christmas Eve, the German soldiers stopped shooting. The soldiers often shouted to each other from one trench to the other, usually shouting insults at one another. Suddenly on Christmas Eve, one of the German soldiers shouted, "Tomorrow you no shoot, we no shoot."

The English soldiers heard the Germans singing the carol "Stille Nacht" which they knew in English as "Silent Night" and they also started to sing carols.

All along the frontline, fighting stopped. The soldiers buried their dead and repaired the trenches. At some parts of the frontline, the soldiers met in No Man's Land. They swapped food, alcohol and tobacco and talked with one

---

1. trenches = Schützengraben

another. At one point, they found a football and hundreds of the men started playing together.

The generals were angry about the **truce**[2]. They thought it was bad for discipline and the men were told to return to the trenches. On Boxing Day, the truce was over and the soldiers started shooting at one another again.

The soldiers took photographs of one another celebrating together and these photographs were sent back to the UK and printed in the newspapers. Although the truce stopped on Boxing Day, one British soldier told the story of a German who was still in the British trenches at New Year! The British soldier was a translator and he was called to go and speak to the German who was drunk and asleep in the British trenches. When the translator arrived, the German soldier had woken up and was standing in the trench holding bottles of beer. He wanted to toast the New Year with the British soldiers. They, however told him he had to go back. At first, he did not want to go. Then they explained that if he stayed, they would have to take him as a prisoner. He did not like that idea either but he was so drunk he could not find his way back to the German trenches on his own. Eventually two British soldiers had to take him across No Man's Land while he **staggered**[3] and sang at the top of his voice.

In a diary which was found years later, German soldier Kurt Zehmisch described what he had experienced. It had been an amazing experience which he had never forgotten. He summed it up with the words: "Christmas, the celebration of Love, managed to bring mortal enemies together as friends for a time."

---

2. truce = Waffenruhe; Waffenstillstand

3. to stagger = torkeln

Good King Wenceslas

20th December

Good King Wenceslas looked out,
on the Feast of Stephen,
When the snow lay round about,
deep and crisp and even;
Brightly shone the moon that night,
tho' the frost was cruel,
When a poor man came in sight,
gath'ring winter fuel.

Most traditional Christmas carols are about Jesus' birth. There is one famous exception, however, which is all about an early medieval ruler in what is now the Czech Republic. His name was King Wenceslas.

Wenceslas was not actually a king. He was the ruler of Bohemia and he was born around 907. His grandfather was the first Christian ruler in the country and Wenceslas was very close to his Christian grandmother, Ludmilla who taught him to read and write. Wenceslas' father died when he was just 13 and his mother took the role of ruler. She was supported by the pagan people in society and she did not like her mother-in-law. She made sure that Ludmilla had no contact with her son. She later even had her killed, making her the country's first Christian martyr.

Wenceslas fought his mother's army and won. He united Bohemia and Moravia: He stopped the persecution of Christians and encouraged education. He also made an agreement with his powerful neighbour, Saxon King Henry I. Bohemia was thus under German rule but kept most of its independence. The people did not like this at all. They turned to Wenceslas' brother Boleslav who had Wenceslas killed. He was just 22 years old.

Boleslav turned out to be a good ruler and, sorry for what he had done, he buried his brother in the church of St Vitus in Prague. Pilgrims started to visit the church and soon Wenceslas was made the patron saint of Bohemia. In 985, 28th September was made a feast day to remember him.

The carol about Wenceslas was written by John Mason Neale (1818-1866). He trained to be a priest but struggled with ill health and so could not take over a church. Instead, he looked after an **almshouse**[1]. He worked hard to look after the poor and founded a religious order, the Sisterhood of St Margaret, to help him.

Neale translated a number of hymns from Greek and Latin and wrote a few of his own. His carol about "Good King Wenceslas" is his most famous. The story in the carol almost surely did not happen and it does not actually mention Christmas. The "Feast of Stephen" is on December 26th. The message of the song is the belief which Neale himself lived by. The final lines of the song say:

> You who now will bless the poor,
> shall yourselves find blessing.

---

1. Armenhaus

The Shortest Day

21st December

Today is the shortest day in the year. People in the northern hemisphere have always celebrated the return of light to the darkness. Today you can sit down with a cup of tea and do this crossword to recap on some Christmas vocabulary.

Across

1 these animals pull Santa's sledge

3 this is a traditional Christmas food made with pastry and filled with dried fruit and spices

4 this word can mean Christmas decorations or what we eat with our turkey

7 a small round green vegetable we eat for Christmas Dinner. Children don't usually like them!

10 Brits pull these at Christmas dinner

12 an evergreen plant with red berries

Down

2 this is a play usually performed by children about the birth of Jesus

5 the name of the reindeer with the red nose

6 a small magical person with pointy ears who helps Santa Claus

7 glass balls to hang on the Christmas tree

8 people hang these at the bottom of the bed for Santa to fill with presents

9 a bird most Brits eat at Christmas time

10 a song we sing at Christmas

11 a wild pig

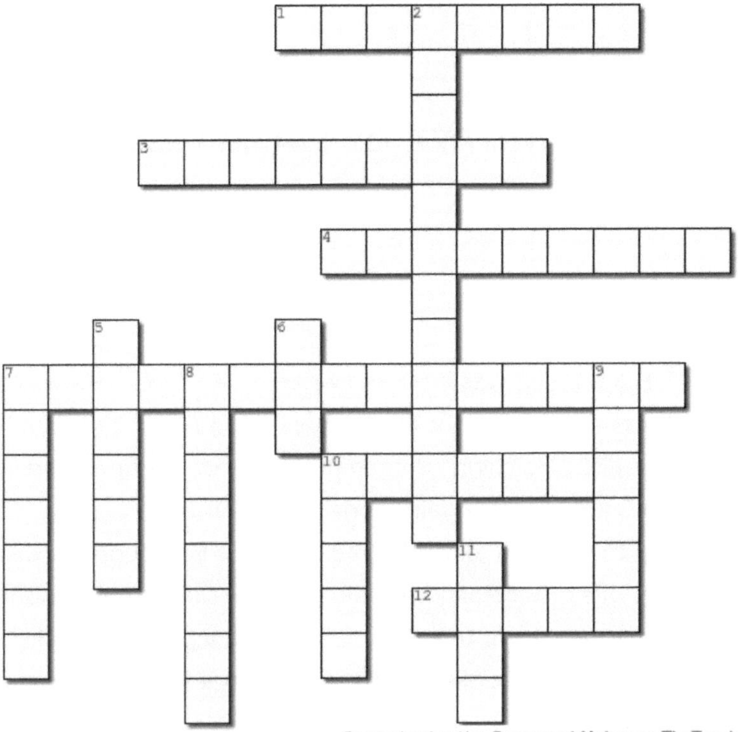

Find the solution at
https://sarahcurtiusbooks.wordpress.com/chr
istmas-crossword/

The Fir Tree by Hans Christian Andersen

22nd December

Hans Christian Andersen was a Danish writer (1805-1875). He wrote novels, poems and plays but is best remembered for his fairy tales. His story about "The Little Matchgirl" is often told at Christmas time. Here is another of Andersen's sad Christmas fairy stories – "The Fir Tree".

Out in the woods, there stood a little fir tree. He had a very good place to grow and got plenty of sunshine and fresh air. Children came to play in the woods and when they saw the fir tree, they said, "What a pretty little tree!". The fir tree did not like that. He looked at all the bigger trees around him and longed to be tall like them.

The years passed and the fir tree grew. In his second winter, there was snow on the ground. A hare ran through the woods and jumped right over the little tree which made him very angry. Nothing made him happy; not the sun or the clouds in the sky or the birds who sang above him. All he wanted was to be tall.

In the autumn, woodcutters came to the wood and **chopped down**[1] some of the tall trees. They fell with a crash and then their branches were chopped off and they were taken out of the wood. In the spring, the fir tree asked a stork if he knew where they were going. The stork thought for a moment and

---

1. to chop down = fällen

then answered, "When I was flying back from Africa, I saw many ships with tall masts. Those masts were fir trees! That is where they are".

The fir tree thought that sounded wonderful. He asked the stork to tell him more about the sea but the stork had already flown off. The sun shone down on the tree and it wished the tree could enjoy his young life. The wind kissed the tree and **dew**[2] settled on his branches but all the fir tree wanted was to grow.

In his third winter, the fir tree saw small trees which were much smaller than him being chopped down and taken away. "Where are they going?" he asked. "They are much smaller and they did not get their branches chopped off."

The sparrows knew the answer. "We have seen them inside houses in the town. They are decorated with apples and gingerbread and toys and candles". The fir tree said he thought that sounded even better than being a mast on a ship. "What happens after they have been decorated like this?" he asked but the sparrows did not know and could not answer him.

Although the air and the sun told him to be happy with his life in the woods, all the fir tree could think about was being taken away and decorated for Christmas. "What is wrong with me? Those trees were much smaller? Why haven't I been taken away? It sounds so wonderful. I would rather be a tree in a home than a mast on a ship".

A year later, the fir tree was one of the first to be cut down. He felt the pain as the axe cut his **trunk**[3]. He was suddenly sad because he knew he would never see the woods and the animals again. When he got to the town, a man pointed at the fir tree and said, "That is a good tree! I'll take that one". Servants came and carried the tree to a very fine house. They stood the fir tree in a big pot filled with sand in a room filled with expensive furniture, with paintings on the walls and a brightly coloured carpet on the floor.

---

2. dew = Tau

3. trunk = Baumstamm

The children and the servants started to decorate the tree with sweets and apples, toys and candles. A big star was placed on the top of his branches and he looked magnificent. The tree was so happy and wondered whether he would grow **roots**[4] in this room and spend the rest of his days covered in these beautiful decorations.

In the evening the candles were lighted. The tree was so excited he shook and a **spark**[5] landed on his branches and he started to burn. The servants quickly put out the fire and the fir tree promised himself that he would stay still from now on. Suddenly the door opened and children ran in, followed by older people. They all stopped and stared at the tree. Then the children started to dance around the tree. After some time, the candles had burned down and then the children started to pull off all the presents.

Now the fir tree realised that no-one was looking at him anymore. They were all busy with the presents. The tree listened as an old man told the children stories. The fir tree was sad because he was no longer decorated but he thought to himself, "Surely they will decorate me again tomorrow".

In the morning, the servants came in. The tree thought they had come to hang pretty things in his branches again but instead the servants pulled him **roughly**[6] out of the room and upstairs. There they threw him into the **attic**[7] and closed the door. The tree lay there for several days and nothing happened.

As he was lying there he started thinking about the woods. It was winter now and there would be snow on the ground. He thought about the hare who jumped over him and all the birds and he felt very lonely indeed.

Then a little mouse came out of its hole and started to climb around in the tree's branches. Another little mouse joined them and asked the tree questions

---

4. roots = Wurzeln

5. spark = Funke

6. rough; roughly = grob, rau

7. attic = Dachboden

about where he had come from. The fir tree told them about his life in the woods. He told them about Christmas and the stories the old man told. The mice thought the tree's stories were wonderful but soon two rats appeared and they said the tree's stories were boring. Soon the mice also got bored and the tree was all alone again. The tree had plenty of time to think and he decided that when he finally saw the light of day again, he would be happy and enjoy his life.

One day men arrived and **dragged**[8] the tree out of the attic. They dragged him down the stairs and into the garden. There were beautiful flowers in the garden. Roses were flowering and **swallows**[9] were flying around. The fir tree loved to feel the sun on his branches again but then he saw that his branches were yellow and dead. The men threw the tree into a corner of the garden which was overgrown with weeds and **nettles**[10] and there he lay.

The children who had danced around the tree came into the garden to play. One of them spotted the tree and saw something shining in the sunshine. The star was still on the top of the tree. The youngest child ran and tore the star off the tree. "Look at this ugly old tree!" he said and gave the tree a kick.

Seeing the fresh flowers in the garden, the tree thought back to his time in the woods, his Christmas in the house and his time with the mice in the attic. "My life is over. I had so much to be happy about but I wasn't and now it is all over."

The gardener came over to the tree and started chopping it up. Soon he was just a pile of fire wood. The wood burned brightly under the pot and sighed deeply, while the little boy danced around with the star, the bright star that the tree had worn on the happiest evening of his life.

---

8. to drag = zerren, schleppen

9. swallow = Schwalbe

10. nettle = Brennnessel

Father Christmas and his Reindeer

23rd December

In Germany, it is the Christ Child who brings the presents on Christmas Eve. In the UK, it is Father Christmas or Santa Claus. Who are these characters and where did they get their names from?

The Puritans banned the celebration of saints' days in the 17th century and Saint Nicholas and his saint's day on 6th December was forgotten. Indeed, Saint Nicholas's Day was never celebrated in the UK in the same ways as in other European countries.

In England, there was a character from the ancient midwinter celebrations. He was dressed in green and represented the coming spring. When giving gifts moved from New Year to Christmas, people began calling this character Father Christmas. In France, he was known as "Père Nöel". In Dickens's story "A Christmas Carol", the ghost of Christmas Present is still described like this ancient figure dressed in green.

Early settlers in the USA, adopted a version of the German "Christkind" and called the person who brought the presents "Kris Kringle". Dutch settlers in the US brought their "Sinterklaas" with them and soon Kris Kringle and Sinterklaas were blended into Santa Claus. In the 20th century, British Father Christmas and Santa Claus also came to be one and the same.

WHY IS SANTA CLAUS' SLEDGE PULLED BY REINDEER?

In 1821, a poem was published in New York called "Old Santeclaus with much delight". This was the first time that Santa Claus had a sledge which was pulled by reindeer. Two years later a poem was published which gave the reindeer names. "A visit from Saint Nicholas" or "'Twas the Night before Christmas" is now read every Christmas Eve by families all over the US. The poem calls the eight reindeer Dasher, Dancer, Prancer, Vixen, Comet, Cupid, Donner and Blitzen. "No Rudolf?" I hear you ask!

Rudolf did not appear until over a hundred years later. In 1939, Robert L. May wrote the story of Rudolf for a department store chain. In 1948, the story was made into a cartoon and in 1949, the famous song was written.

TRUE OR FALSE? SANTA CLAUS IN HIS RED SUIT WAS CREATED BY COCA COLA

False!

Saint Nicholas already wore a red robe as a bishop. The Father Christmas figure in the UK wore green with fur trimmings. In an American magazine in 1863, St Nicholas was shown wearing a Stars and Stripes outfit! The artist who drew the picture, Thomas Nast, drew a picture of Santa every year for the next 20 years. During this time, Santa started to look more and more like he does today, with a red suit and white fur trimming.

In the 1930s, Coca Cola began using a version of Santa who looked very much like the one Nast had drawn. The picture of Santa holding a Coca Cola bottle and his big red truck is now famous throughout the world. But Coca Cola did not invent Santa Claus!

Christmas Eve

24th December

On the final day before Christmas, here is a quiz to see how much you can remember from what you have read.

1. What was the "Butter Letter"? (1st)

2. What is the 26th December called in the United Kingdom? (2nd)

3. What are the New Year's celebrations called in Scotland? (2nd)

4. Under which evergreen plant do people kiss? (3rd)

5. Which country gives the UK a Christmas tree which is put up in Trafalgar Square in London? (3rd)

6. What was the 6th January called in the Middle Ages? (4th)

7. What is the name of the festival which the Vikings celebrated in midwinter? (4th)

8. Who wrote the "Elves and the Shoemaker"? (5th)

9. Where was Saint Nicholas a bishop? (6th)

10. In the Tudor period, when did people give each other presents? (7th)

11. Who banned Christmas? (7th)

12. When were the first Christmas cards sent? (8th)

13. Who was called the "Pudding King"? (9th)

14. Who wrote the story "A Christmas Carol"? (9th)

15. Who printed the first collection of Christmas Carols in England? (10th)

16. In the carol "The Twelve Days of Christmas", what did my true love sent to me on the fifth day of Christmas? (11th)

17. Where did the pretty poinsettia plant originally grow? (12th)

18. Which Christmas drink is made with eggs? (15th)

19. Which fruit is used to make a Christingle? (16th)

20. What three things would you find in a Christmas cracker? (17th)

21. Which King of England was crowned on Christmas Day in 1066? (18th)

22. What did some Scottish students steal in 1950? (18th)

23. Which game did the British and German soldiers play together on Christmas Day in 1914? (19th)

24. Where did King Wenceslas rule? (21st)

Find the answers in the book or here:
https://sarahcurtiusbooks.wordpress.com/christmas-quiz-solutions/

Celtic Christmas Blessing

May you be blessed
with the Spirit of the season,
which is peace.
The gladness of the season,
which is hope.
And the heart of the season,
which is love.

ALSO BY SARAH CURTIUS

WHO ARE YOU CALLING OLD?

WHO ARE YOU
CALLING OLD?

SARAH CURTIUS

How old is 'old'? Do *you* feel old? What happens to us as we get older? Read about some inspiring people and find out about what happens in our brain as we age and why learning new skills is still possible. (CEFR Level B1)

ISBN: 978-3-7543-3070-8

SHAKESPEARE: STORIES FOR TODAY

In this book you will find stories based on Shakespeare's plays and his characters. Meet Bottom from "A Midsummer Night's Dream", the young lovers from "The Merchant of Venice", and the twins separated after a shipwreck from "Twelfth Night". (CEFR Level B1/B2)

ISBN: 978-3-756-832-552

Shakespeare
STORIES FOR TODAY
Sarah Curtius

Order the books in your local bookshop or here
https://www.bod.de/buchshop/catalogsearch/result/
index/?q=Sarah+Curtius&bod_pers_id=13959116

COMING SOON

W^{ALES}

A book about Wales, a land rich with history, myths and legends, written for English learners (CEFR Level B1).

What languages do people speak in Wales?

Who was the first Prince of Wales?

What is the position of Wales in the United Kingdom?

And find out about famous Welsh people you did not realise were Welsh!

COMING 2023

THE HISTORY SERIES

Books about the history of the United Kingdom for English learners (CEFR Level B1).

As well as rulers, we will learn about what was happening in science and culture, aspects of every day life in different eras and find out about a scandal or two.

The first book in the series will look at the times of the **Tudor Kings**.

Who are the Tudors?

Who was the first woman to publish a book?

Who invented the first watch?

Acknowledgements

Thank you once again to Christoph and Iona for proofreading and to Iona for the chapter about Saint Nicholas. Thanks to Annakiska for your input and proofreading skills!

Thank you to all my family – Mum, Christoph, Iona and Debbi – for many wonderful Christmases!

Image Credits:

Cover image: AdobeStock, netrun78
Header: AdobeStock, World of Vector
p7 holly (Pixabay, suju-foto); ivy (Pixabay, suju-foto);
p8 laurel (Pixabay, ulleo)
p35 AdobeStock, scott
p43 crossword created using The Crossword Maker on
TheTeachersCorner.net
p 63 AdobeStock, Good Studio